Life With God

Basics for New Christians

Helen Johns

Evangel Publishing House

Nappanee, Indiana 46550

Cover photograph: Jupiterimages Corporation © 2006

Cover design: Matthew Gable

Library of Congress Catalog Card Number: 96-85027

ISBN-10: 0-916035-23-9

ISBN-13: 978-0-916035-23-5

Spanish edition also available:
La Vida con Dios: Elementos Básicos para los Creyentes Nuevos

ISBN-10: 0-916035-30-1

ISBN-13: 978-0-916035-30-3

PHOTOTYPESET ⚫ FOR QUALITY

Printed in the United States of America

10 9 8 7 6 5 4

Contents

Introduction

In this book, you will find help for beginning your Christian life. You may want to read it all in one sitting, or take several days or weeks to absorb what's here.

You undoubtedly will need guidance as you start your adventure as a Christian. The questions in the "Talk It Over" sections near the end of each chapter are intended for you to discuss with a friend or pastor.

The "Check It Out" Bible search questions may be done on your own or with a friend or a group. (Don't peek at the answers in the back of the book until you have tried your best to answer on your own. You'll grow a lot faster if you let God be your teacher.)

Some good verses to memorize are found on various pages. Practical hints are printed in boxes.

1

New Life!

If you are reading this book, you likely have made the most important decision a person can make. By confessing faith in Jesus Christ, you have taken the first step into a new life. You have begun a personal relationship with the Creator of the universe. You are his. You even have a new name—Christian—and are ready to begin a wonderful adventure.

Just in case it all doesn't seem real, let's look back for a moment at where you have been. Then we'll focus on where you are going.

Why did you come to Christ?

Perhaps one of the following descriptions fits you.

A search for purpose. Some people go through life immersed in activities and plans, only to realize one day that they have no good reason for what they are doing. When we come to know Christ, we start to find answers for questions such as, "Why am I alive?" or "Is there any purpose for my life?" We find purpose in God's plan for us and for the Church. We can begin to live fully and abundantly because of Jesus.

Emptiness. Some people are afraid of being alone. When the TV goes off, the party is over, the work is done, or the family leaves the nest, they feel a hollowness inside. A man named

Augustine has said that in each of us is a God-shaped vacuum. Jesus comes inside and fills that space in us that yearns for him. He is our constant friend and companion. We no longer need to fear being alone. If we have previously felt unloved or unlovely, he begins to fill our lives with his love.

Fear of death. Some people rarely give a thought to dying. Then one day a friend or family member dies, or the person is in a near-fatal accident. Suddenly the seeming finality of death or the fear of separation envelopes us and we are terrorized by the unknown. Only the Christian knows the reality of the promise of eternal life with God. Because Christ rose from the dead, we too shall live.

Confusion. In our world there are too many philosophies, too many choices. We search and search for Truth after which we can pattern our lives. Many ideas make some sense, but don't really help in the long run. The Christian knows that Jesus is the Way, the Truth, and the Life. He helps us put all the puzzle pieces together.

Restlessness, constant turmoil. Do you know someone who is constantly rowing upstream? He may be trying by his good works, morality, or religious practices to attain enough "goodness" to get to God. This person is plagued by a list of "do's and don'ts" a mile long, but never can seem to measure up to his own standards. Peace with God, with mankind, and with oneself are promises for those who walk with Christ. There is no longer any need to fight uphill battles all the time.

The trap of self-sufficiency. Do you know people who vow to change, but never can make it stick? They may know how to turn their life over to Christ, but are afraid, too stubborn, or see no need. They flounder along on their own, flitting from one courtroom to the next, from lover to lover, or from temper tantrum to the next angry fit. "I'm going to get my life straightened out, then I'll say yes to Christ" or "Let me stop my bad habits, then I'll come to church" or "My life is O.K. Why do I need God?" Christians learn to give their lives—faults *and* successes—to Jesus. As we allow God more and more control over our decisions and actions, he helps us become more like Christ.

Desperation. We all know persons who have lost hope because of various circumstances. Perhaps their families or finances are falling apart, and depression and anxiety have driven them to desperate acts. Christians learn that God is an available God, willing to help in times of great trouble. The Bible says that God is a rock and a hiding place, a place of strength and shelter.

Past sins. Then there are people who feel that they have done such terrible things that they cannot become a Christian. They have the false idea that people need to be "good" before God will accept them. The wonderful news is that God forgives us when we turn away from sin and come to Christ in faith. He no longer holds our sins against us.

Have you seen yourself in any of these descriptions? If so, you are not alone. Many before you have experienced similar situations and attitudes. We all have sinned—every one of us. But you are now in the company of all those who have been redeemed. God has reached to you, and you to him. You now can look ahead with confidence.

What's ahead?

Did you know that God has been waiting for you? The Bible says that you and I have wandered around aimlessly like sheep needing a shepherd. God values you and me, cherishing us as persons of immeasurable worth. Patiently God called us to him until we came.

At first, we all come to God full of faults and weaknesses. Even if we have deeply offended him in the past by our thoughts and actions, God has been ready to forgive and give to us abundantly from all the riches that are his. Salvation and all its benefits are a free gift from God.

Adopted! You now have a heavenly Father who is willing to give to you all the privileges of being a son or daughter. He will protect and love you. Because you are his child, you have a new heart and spirit. You are part of a new family, with Christians as your brothers and sisters. It is a vigorous, growing family because God—who *is* love—is at its head.

Now, having God's riches does not necessarily mean discovering the pot of gold at the end of the rainbow. God's riches are peace, joy, hope, self-control, assurance, faith . . . and a host of things money cannot buy. As we seek to follow Christ, he gradually and consistently showers us with all we need to be happy in him. It does not mean we won't have troubles. But it does mean we now have the same power Jesus had to cope with life and the same loving father to guide us.

Forgiven. It doesn't matter what you've done or failed to do before. You now are forgiven. Your sins are erased when you accept Christ; they don't have to haunt you anymore. You can be rid of the guilt and of the sick, angry feelings. You are saved by faith and are free to begin again. New life! It means a brand new start.

Then, as we trust Jesus day by day, we no longer need to carry the heavy load of trying to "be good" on our own. Though Christians try hard to please God because we love him, we all sin and fall short of his expectations. But as we turn to God when we fail, he forgives us and helps us change. Christians have this special privilege because Jesus suffered our punishment for us.

Changed. When you gave your life to Jesus, a thrilling thing happened. The Holy Spirit—the presence of God now on earth—came to live *in you.* The Spirit is helping, guiding, teaching, and comforting. You will increasingly learn how to listen to the Spirit talk to you. But for now, rest assured that the Spirit will—as you allow—create in you several new desires. Perhaps you recognize some of them already. Others will come over time as you become more like Christ.

1. One of these desires is a hunger for the Bible, God's Word. This hunger means not being satisfied until you know God better. You will want to read the Bible and pray. You will want to be in church where the action is with God's people. You will want to know Christ intimately so you can be like him in every way.

2. Another desire will be to keep God's commands. The Spirit will give you such gratitude for God's sacrifice of his Son for you, that you will want to please God. His rules will no longer seem like a list of burdensome "don'ts." It will be increasingly

*"I consider everything a loss
compared to the surpassing greatness
of knowing Christ Jesus my Lord."*

Philippians 3:8

obvious to you as you walk with Christ that God's boundaries are his way of loving and protecting you. You will want to obey him.

3. You also will experience a growing love for Christians— those persons you previously may have thought were pesky, strange, or radical. You will see that they—though far from perfect—are Christ's representatives on earth. They are your brothers and sisters. You will want to be with them, learn from them, work with them, and even laugh and cry with them. Enjoy your new family, starting right away.

4. Moreover, you will have an increasing concern and compassion for all people. You will find yourself forgiving someone who hurts you, giving money to someone who is hungry, choosing peaceful solutions instead of violence, and a variety of other responses not typical of the previous you. You will see people in a different light and you will want to tell others about this wonderful Jesus who is changing your life. You have a new understanding. You have found the key to a great mystery and will want to share it.

Eternal life. God's greatest gift is eternal life. Even though our bodies will die, there is a part of us which will live on in heaven until Christ returns to earth. We then will be reunited with our bodies and live forever with God. This promise—reserved for Christians—is our source of ultimate hope. Eternal life begins the moment we confess our sins and believe on Jesus.

Be assured of this: because of your confession of faith, you have stepped onto a new path with God. You may be experiencing a range of emotions and questions. Or it is possible that you aren't "feeling" much at all. You may not be able to touch or see anything, but *new life has begun in you.* It has because God says so. His Word is true.

As the days and weeks and months go by, you will find evidences of God's dwelling with you. Believe it! Enjoy it! Get ready to grow!

Bible Study Tips

If you have not looked up Bible verses before, here are some tips:

1. The New International Version (NIV) is a plainly worded Bible, and would be a good one to use for these questions. However, almost any Bible you have is O.K. to start with.
2. In most Bibles, the 66 books are listed in a table of contents in the front. You may look for the page numbers there.
3. The Bible is divided into two major sections. After the reference for each question, you will see either OT for Old Testament (the first and larger section) or NT for New Testament.
4. You may want to try looking up the passages without using the table of contents. After some of the questions, you will find a hint on how to find the correct book.
5. Don't become discouraged. After a little practice, you will wonder why using your Bible ever seemed difficult at all!

As you will learn in the next chapter, an essential of your new life is reading and studying the Bible. Stop reading now and answer the questions that follow. Or, you may choose to go on to Chapter 2 and return at a later time to the questions, either by yourself or with a friend.

☑ Check It Out

1. If anyone is in Christ, he (she) is a _____
   _____ ; the old one has gone, the new has
   come! (2 Corinthians 5:17 NT)

2. God will (a) _____ us with power
   through the Holy Spirit so that we will understand how much
   God (b) _____ us. (Ephesians 3:16-19 NT)

3. One of the gifts God can give us is _____.
   (John 14:27 NT. John is one of the first four books of the NT
   called the Gospels.)

4. A person who believes in Jesus as Savior and Lord has
   _____ _____ . (John 3:16 NT)

5. Those who come to Jesus will have _____.
   (Matthew 11:28 NT)

continued on next page

6. God can help us get over our _____ . (Psalm 34:4 OT. If you open your Bible close to the center, you probably will be near the book of Psalms.)

7. If we confess our sins, God is faithful and just and will _____ _____ . (1 John 1:9 NT. This book is different from the Gospel of John. Look toward the end of the NT.)

8. Because of his (a) _____ for us, we are now called (b) _____ of (c) _____ . (1 John 3:1 NT)

9. We can be sure we have come to Christ if we:
   (1 John 2:3 NT) (a) _____
   (1 John 3:11) (b) _____
   (1 John 4:13) (c) _____

"If anyone acknowledges that Jesus is the Son of God, God lives in him and he in God."

1 John 4:15

Talk It Over

1. What circumstances led to your coming to Christ? Try to describe the "old you"—your desires, goals, and problems. Then try to pinpoint any evidences of the "new you" that already may be showing.

2. Think about the following prayer of repentance and salvation or the one that you prayed. Is there anything in it that is unclear to you?

   Lord Jesus, I need you. Thank you for dying on the cross for my sins. I am sorry for all my sins. I open the door of my life and receive you as my Savior and Lord. Thank you for forgiving my sins and giving me eternal life. Take control of my life. Make me the kind of person you want me to be.

3. How does it make you feel to know that God has (a) adopted you, (b) forgiven you, (c) given you the Holy Spirit, (d) given you eternal life?

4. Pray a short prayer. (a) Thank God for creating you; (b) tell God you love him; (c) thank God for Jesus and eternal life; (d) ask God to help you grow as a Christian.

By now you are sure something has happened, but you need help to know what to do next. In the following chapters, we introduce you to four basic needs of every Christian: prayer, Bible study, fellowship, and worship. These are definite steps you can take to start (and keep on in) your Christian journey. The more time you spend doing these things, the more you will grow and develop your friendship with God and experience his blessings.

2

Prayer

What is it?

Very simply, prayer is dialogue with God. As in any loving relationship with a good friend, our closeness with God increases the more we talk with him. God and the person praying both benefit. But this interaction is as necessary as breathing for the Christian. Jesus himself gave us an example by regularly being with God in prayer.

Because you have become a Christian, you now have the privilege of talking directly with the great God of the universe. God communicates with you through such means as the Bible, preaching, Christian friends, and the promptings of the Holy Spirit in your thought life. In response, you may approach God boldly in Jesus' name. It is because of who *Christ* is that God will listen, not because of what *we* have done.

Why pray?

A great part of the reason for prayer is the strengthening of our relationship with our heavenly Father. Being with him gives us joy. Prayer satisfies a deep need of our hearts to be close to him. It is also a means of discovering God's guidance, and is his way of alleviating our worries. In prayer, we receive the power to resist evil and temptation. When we spend time with God, we become more like him.

Another reason for prayer is that God wants to change things on earth through us. When we pray, *we* change. Our hateful attitudes change to love; we gain the resolve to stop our harmful actions. Moreover, the prayers of Christians move God to influence circumstances. If you have not experienced it already, you will soon see situations change because of the prayers of Christian people.

How should I pray?

Remember first that dialogue involves talking *and* listening. When you talk with someone, you usually don't need to follow a set pattern or use fancy words. You don't necessarily need to talk about lofty subjects or do all the talking. The same is true in prayer. Talk to God about the small things as well as the big. God wants to hear what is on your mind, and will never condemn you if you *honestly* express yourself and *humbly* are willing to listen and change in return. Even if your prayers are not expressed perfectly, the Holy Spirit helps them sound all right to God.

When you pray, stop for awhile, clearing the way for God to speak to you with a still, small voice. Someone you know may be hurting and God might prompt you with the thought, "Pick up the phone and call." You may have made plans for the day, but God instructs, "Change them." You may have some unknown sin, and God will say, "Go confess and make it right with that person." God also can bring comfort and peace in moments of silence. Stillness on our part allows God his part in the conversation.

Pray often. Do it in church and out; by yourself and with others; in small groups or public worship. Include praises, thanks, and confession of sins. Tell God of your needs and the needs of others. Try one-sentence prayers in the car, the office, or

*"Do not be anxious about anything,
but in everything, by prayer and petition,
with thanksgiving,
present your requests to God."*

Philippians 4:6

the grocery. Schedule prolonged prayer in the quiet of your regularly-set-aside devotions time. (We'll talk more about this in Chapter 5.) Be specific in your requests. Do it on your knees or in the shower. Pray silently or at the top of your lungs in song. But be sure to pray!

Will there be results?

What about unanswered prayer? While prayers seldom truly go unanswered (the answer may be yes, no, or wait), the Bible tells us several reasons why prayers might be ineffective. If that would happen to you sometime, check yourself on these points: Am I holding on to unconfessed sin? Have I not forgiven someone and therefore have a broken relationship? Do I really believe God can do what I'm asking? Or am I asking for something clearly unbiblical, something my heavenly Father knows is not good for me?

The better you come to know God, the more you will find joy and results in praying. If you would like, try writing down what you pray about. Then record and date the answers. (There is space to start on page 60.) You will be amazed at God's faithfulness. It is a tremendous source of comfort and confidence to know that our prayers are being presented to God by Christ himself.

☑ Check It Out

1. Because of Jesus, we can now approach God in prayer with _____ in prayer. (Hebrews 4:16 NT. Watch out! This book sounds like it ought to be in the OT. You will understand verse 16 better if you read verses 14 and 15 also.)

2. Instead of being (a) _____, we should pray. If we do, God promises us his (b) _____. (Philippians 4:6-7 NT. Like many other books in the NT, this one is a letter named after the people to whom it was written.)

3. God the father is eager to give his children _____ _____. (Matthew 7:9-12 NT)

4. We can have confidence of receiving from God what we ask, when we (a) _____, and (b) _____ him. (1 John 3:21-22 NT)

5. From Matthew 6:6, Matthew 18:19-20, and Acts 1:13-14 (all NT), we learn that it is O.K. to pray (a) _____, in a (b) _____ group, and in a (c) _____ group.

6. Prayer can keep us from falling into _____. (Matthew 26:41)

7. In the Bible, we find Jesus praying at what times of day?

Mark 1:35 NT (a) ⎯⎯⎯⎯⎯⎯⎯⎯⎯⎯⎯⎯⎯⎯⎯⎯⎯

Mark 6:46-47 (b) ⎯⎯⎯⎯⎯⎯⎯⎯⎯⎯⎯⎯⎯⎯⎯⎯⎯

Luke 6:12 NT (c) ⎯⎯⎯⎯⎯⎯⎯⎯⎯⎯⎯⎯⎯⎯⎯⎯⎯

 Talk It Over

1. Is there anything about these ideas that is new to you?
   —We can talk to God as a friend.
   —Part of prayer is listening.
   —*We* change when we pray.
   —It's O.K. to pray anywhere about anything.

2. Think about how you want to start your prayer life.
   —Will you set a special time each day?
   —Will you find a prayer partner?
   —Will you record your prayers in a notebook and watch for answers?

3. Read and discuss the prayer in Matthew 6:5-13.

3

Bible Study

Studying the Bible is the best way to know God. When we open the Scriptures, we are reading more than a textbook. The Bible is God's revelation of himself and the story of his Son, Jesus Christ. We should read the Bible with reverence and expectation. God inspired the many different writers, over a period of hundreds of years, to speak personally to you and me. It is not only our handbook for living, but the way to know the mind of Almighty God.

Can the Bible make sense to me?

Perhaps you have tried to read the Bible before and it was impossible to understand. You may have thought it was dull and contradictory. If you own a Bible, it might be in a dusty corner, or just a coffee table decoration. But now that you are a Christian, you will begin to read the Bible with new understanding. The Holy Spirit is now in you to teach you and clarify the meaning.

As you read, you will be amazed at how the Bible will start to make sense. At first, it may seem like a puzzle with many, many pieces. But one by one, with prayer and diligent searching, the pieces will start fitting together. You will begin to see how perfect God's Word is, each shape intricately woven into the next.

Studying the Bible is a lifetime adventure. The puzzle may not be completed until we see Jesus in heaven. But on earth, as we read his book, we are amazed at who God is. When we set aside time daily to be with God in his Word, God helps us to grow in behavior and understanding. Each nugget of truth is precious.

How do I start?

There are several ways to learn from the Bible. A balanced combination of these methods will help you grow.

Hearing. Jesus used to go to the top of a hill, or sit in a boat and preach to the people. The Apostle Paul would stand in the town square and tell about Jesus while the people listened. Today, with all kinds of sophisticated means of communication, opportunities are more numerous than ever to hear the Word. The best way is in your local congregation. Your church may have services mid-week and Sunday evening as well as Sunday morning. Take advantage of every such opportunity to hear about Jesus. Listen carefully to sermons. Take notes and review them during the week.

Another way is Christian radio and TV. Let your pastor help you carefully select good programs with reputable speakers so that your hearing of the Scriptures through music and preaching can be more than a Sunday-only event. A word of caution: exposure to the Word in this way is often helpful and inspiring, but could become confusing and can never take the place of your local congregation.

Daily reading. Some people set a goal of reading all the way through the Bible in a year. But you need to find a pace comfortable for your schedule. By reading only a few chapters a day, you can gain an overview of the Bible. Many sources publish guides to daily reading. (One plan is printed on page 58.) You are wise to follow one of these instead of starting at Genesis and plowing through to the end. Let your pastor or Christian friend help you devise a reasonable plan and find a translation that suits you. Then set aside a special time each day to read. Don't worry if you don't understand every word. Take in what you can.

---

*"These are written that you may believe
that Jesus is the Christ, the Son of God,
and that by believing
you may have life in his name."*

John 20:31

Study. As you learn how to study the Bible, you will be amazed that almost every word contains a treasure chest of meaning. Unraveling the truths of Scripture takes study skills that will grow over a lifetime. Don't expect to be good at it right away. One of the best ways to start is in a small group setting. There are group and home Bible studies available in many churches. Or perhaps you have a special friend who would take time to study and discuss the Bible with you. Also, attend Sunday school regularly, choosing the class that studies directly from the Bible. Within such settings, you will find a variety of kinds of Bible study. Each one is a different and valuable way to learn.

Application. There is a big difference between *knowing* God and knowing *about* God. Hours of study are useless if you fail to ask yourself, "How does this speak to me?" It is essential that in the quiet of your heart, you ask God to reveal to you what your response to his Word should be. It is possible—even probable—that each person might come away from a Bible passage with a different personal application. That does not mean that our understandings are different. It means that God has marvelous ways of applying the Bible to our individual circumstances and maturity. What is important is to measure our lives by the standard of God's Word.

Mark and memorize. As you read and study, you will find special verses which almost jump off the page and say, "This is for you!" Don't be afraid to write in your Bible. Underline those verses and put a date and notes in the margin. They will be a reminder in the future of how and when God spoke to you. Don't be afraid to wear out your Bible. The pages may get frayed, but your life will change for the better.

As you find passages which speak to you, copy and memorize them. Put them on your refrigerator, nightstand, desk, or breakfast table. Let them sink into your heart. They will remain there as guidance, protection, and encouragement as you face each day. Christians often say that in difficult circumstances the Holy Spirit has brought to their mind verses of strength and comfort memorized years before.

The Bible will bring you a lifetime of joy and challenge. Investing your time in the Scripture will bring you rich dividends. It is your daily spiritual food. Plan to start today.

☑ Check It Out

1. Non-Christians cannot understand and accept the wisdom of God. To them, the Bible seems like _____.
(1 Corinthians 2:14 NT. There are two letters to the Corinthians. Look in the first one.)

2. God's thoughts are _____ than our thoughts. (Isaiah 55:8-9 OT. Isaiah is a few books past Psalms.)

3. All Scripture is (a) _____,
and is useful for (b) _____ , (c) _____
_____ , (d) _____, and
(e) _____ . (2 Timothy 3:16 NT)

4. Even the _____ didn't understand all that Jesus said. (Luke 9:43-45 NT)

5. Yet when we believe in Christ, he _____ our minds and helps us understand the Scriptures. (Luke 24:45 NT)

6. Who is with us to help us understand the Bible? _____ _____ (John 16:13 NT)

7. A good prayer to pray before Bible study is: "_____ _____ _____ ." (Psalm 119:18 OT)

8. Why should we "hide the Word in our heart"? (memorize Scripture) (Psalm 119:9-11 OT) _____

9. We should not only read the Bible, but _____ what it says. (James 1:22-25 NT)

 Talk It Over

1. There are many translations of the Bible. If you have not already done so, look over several and decide with a friend which is best for you.
2. Discuss the different kinds of writings in the Bible such as letters to persons and churches, history books, poetry, books of the law, prophecy, etc. Discuss how the whole Bible—Genesis to Revelation—is really the story of Jesus.
3. Think about how you would like to start studying the Bible. Consider the suggestions in this chapter.

4

Fellowship

Now that you are a Christian, you have a new family—the biggest extended family in the world. You have a long, rich family history which includes every believer in Christ throughout history. You have hundreds of thousands of brothers and sisters right now—Christians all around the world. Realizing your heritage, you will want to begin an association with a local congregation. This new family will become a major source of wonderful experiences for you, and the place for you to grow into the person God wants you to be.

Can I get along without going to church?

One of the first things to realize is that "going to church" is not merely a matter of getting up on Sunday morning and sitting in a pew. Being part of church life means *belonging* and *participating*. It involves a total giving of yourself to the reasons for and purposes of the body of believers. Let's take a look at why this is so.

The Church is Christ's body. The Bible says that as Christians we are all part of Christ's body on earth. It is impossible for us to live and function apart from the rest of the body. We can compare Christ's body to our own. If we are a toe, for instance, we can't say to the eye or the hand, "I don't need you." We need to be connected to survive.

God commands participation. If for no other reason, we want to be with believers because God commands it. You will recall that the Holy Spirit is working within you to give you the right desires. One of these is to be with Christians on a regular basis. Don't resist the Spirit's nudgings. Go!

Fellowship is a privilege. Remember that God desires the best for us. So he gave us the New Testament example of community life—the church—to insure our care, growth, and contentment. If before you became a Christian you feared rejection, the church is the place to seek acceptance. If your life was full of strife and broken relationships, you will find friendship and skills for being with people. If you were hurt, you will find healing. . . . Christians, though not perfect, are Christ's embodiment—his representatives—on earth. You can go to them for wisdom and love. Churches have a variety of people and programs to meet your needs.

You have a responsibility. Christians respond to the love of Christ and his church by returning that love. By submitting to one another in service, we gratefully return part of what God has so graciously given us. No member is any less important than the rest. *You* are necessary and will find the abilities God has given you for the building of his church. Don't expect people to continue to urge you to come to church as they may have done before you became a Christian. *You take the initiative* to find your gifts, to love and to serve.

What will happen when I go?

First, you will find people who are pleased that you have come to the Lord in faith. They will not embarrass you, but will try the best way they know to make you feel at home. Christians who are daily aware of God's love for them will accept you as part of the family because you now love the Lord just as they do. As

"We know that we have passed from death to life, because we love our brothers."

1 John 3:14

"Dear friends, let us love one another, for love comes from God."

1 John 4:7

you reveal to them the changes in you and how God is present in your life, you can expect them to be excited for and with you.

In the closeness of life together in the local church, we are changed. We learn and interpret God's Word together; we strive to live obediently; we gently warn and correct one another; we practice Christlikeness by forgiving, loving, and sharing everything, from earthly possessions to tears and laughter; we carry each other's burdens; we find a oneness and a joy only found among Christians. It's a great experience.

Now, if this picture of the church doesn't quite match yours, remember that Christians are human beings with choices and faults. Author Anne Ortlund says, "Every congregation has a choice to be one of two things, . . . a bag of marbles, single units that don't affect each other in collision . . . or a bag of grapes. The juices begin to mingle, and there's no way to extricate yourselves if you tried. Each is part of all."* This "oneness" is part of God's plan. Ultimately we change for the better through close interaction with other Christians.

---

*Anne Ortlund, *Up With Worship*, (Regal Books, Ventura, Calif. 93006, revised edition, 1982), p. 102.

Your local congregation will likely encourage you to follow certain procedures: a membership class, personal public testimony, and baptism and communion. It pleased God to give us the pattern for such activities. You should enter into them with open heart and mind, realizing that these are privileges. They are the visible means of the church declaring its love and devotion to you, and your means of publicly identifying with and committing yourself to the church. Delight in these steps of faith without fear.

You will also find that most congregations have all kinds of opportunities aside from worship. Attend everything you can. Jump in feet first and become part of what is going on in ministry, outreach, fun, business meetings, worship, and prayer. With the guidance of your pastor and other Christians, find your place of service, and enjoy the benefits of life in Christ's body.

Sunday Tips

1. Plan for Sunday on Saturday night. Study your Sunday school lesson; lay out your clothes; bathe the children; set your alarm; go to bed early.

2. Plan a simple meal for Sunday noon so you can be attentive all through the service and not worry about the food.

3. Attend Sunday school as well as church. Stay for fellowship meals even if you didn't remember to bring anything.

4. Inquire about a nursery or junior church for your children. Don't leave them at home. Take along a few items of diversion for small children if they need to stay with you.

5. Linger after the service and look for opportunities to encourage the pastor and other believers.

☑ Check It Out

1. God's purpose in unifying us in the church is so that all of us, with one heart (mind) and voice, will _____ the God and Father of our Lord Jesus Christ. (Romans 15:5-6 NT. Paul wrote this letter to the Roman Christians.)

2. We should meet together so we can _____ one another. (Hebrews 10:25 NT)

3. What was the early church seen doing in all of these Scriptures? Acts 1:6; Acts 2:1; Acts 4:31; Acts 12:12; Acts 15:30; 1 Corinthians 5:4 (all NT) _____

4. We are all parts of Christ's _____ . (Romans 12:5 NT)

5. God gives us certain functions and abilities for the benefit of the church. List as many as you can. (Romans 12:6-8; 1 Corinthians 12:8-10; and Ephesians 4:11 NT) _____

   _____

   _____

   _____

   _____

6. The purpose of these gifts is so that the church will reach unity and become _____ , like Christ. (Ephesians 4:13 NT)

continued on next page

7. People will know that we are Christians if we:

(John 13:35 NT) (a) _____

(1 Peter 3:8-9 NT) (b) _____

(Galatians 6:2 NT) (c) _____

 **Talk It Over**

1. How would you describe your attitude before you came to Christ about people who go to church? How has it changed?

2. Do you have any fears about being with God's family? Talk them over.

3. What changes might you need to make in your life so that you can be faithful in attending the services and activities of the church?

4. Have a Christian friend describe to you the good things his or her church has to offer you. What can you offer the congregation?

5

Worship

Worship is the result of a deep hunger to be with God and other Christians. As we express this desire for closeness to God verbally and in actions, God draws near to us. The Apostle Paul said, "I want to know Christ." Behind these words was a consuming passion not only to be in God's presence, but to be engulfed by the love which flows between us and God. As we adore him and empty ourselves of the concerns of the world and our self-centeredness, God fills us with his joy and strength.

Worship takes two different forms: our private devotions, and group (corporate) worship services. Both are necessary as we walk in faith.

Private worship

We have already discussed the two major elements of private devotions: prayer and Bible study. Private times are opportunities for communication with God. We can lay aside the cares of the day and be with him. God strengthens, teaches, forgives, and equips us for facing the world. Devotional moments are also the fulfillment of one of our purposes for being alive: to honor God.

Time and place. Find a time that suits you. Some say that the best time is early in the morning before the distractions of the day overwhelm you. Regardless of when, find a place of quiet solitude, free from interruptions. Give the Lord your undivided attention at a time when you are alert and thinking clearly.

Meet God. Many people follow this or a similar pattern for their devotions: a prayer expressing a desire for God's presence; a Scripture reading; and meditation, seeking application to their own life. Over the years you will develop various ways to have devotions. At some point, you may want to obtain a devotional guide chosen with the help of your pastor. As you read what others have written and follow their patterns for study, your thoughts will be directed toward God. You will learn the experiences and insights of other Christians as examples and models for your own spiritual journey.

But don't confuse *reading about God* with *being with God.* While devotional books and study guides whet our appetite for God and teach us many important things, they are no substitute for actually meeting God through prayer and reading the Bible. Be careful that you desire a close encounter of the life-changing kind, and that you don't substitute other people's experiences for your own.

Drudgery or delight? Often we enter our devotions time with a sense of expectation and leave with a spirit of delight. But it may not happen that way every time. Sometimes we give our time to God out of desire and sometimes out of obedience. (The longer we are Christians, the more these motivations mesh. When we choose to do the right thing, that often leads to happiness.) But we need not feel discouraged or guilty if bells don't ring or cymbals crash every time we pray and study. Some days, you will be overjoyed by new insight or a direction from the Holy Spirit. Other days, it will be enough to know that you have met in quiet with a faithful God who is there for you just because you approached him. Don't judge your devotional time by your emotional reaction to it. Judge it by whether you have come to God with pure motives and a desire to know him better. God has been with you whether you feel it or not.

Persist. If you find that you have difficulty setting aside a regular time for devotions, don't give up. Or if you become weary

"Praise the Lord, O my soul;
all my inmost being, praise his holy name.
Praise the Lord, O my soul,
and forget not all his benefits."

Psalm 103:1-2

of the same routine, change the pattern of your devotional time. Perhaps you need to find a prayer partner. Study and pray together long enough to spark new interest. Or keep a journal. Make an entry about what you are feeling and thinking. Then write down your prayer for the day. Or before you study, make a list of questions you may have for God and come back days later to see how he has answered. Whatever you do, keep at it. God desires this time with you and will reward you.

Corporate worship

The Psalm writer David wrote, "One thing I have asked from the Lord, . . . that I may dwell in the house of the Lord all the days of my life, to behold the beauty of the Lord, and meditate in his temple" (Psalm 27:4). David's deepest desire was to be in God's house for worship. As Christians, we have the privilege of coming together as the church. The New Testament makes it clear that this group worship gives an added dimension to our private devotion.

In Revelation, the last book of the Bible, we see a thrilling picture of worship. All Christians will someday be gathered in heaven, a great multitude crying out, "Holy, holy, holy" in celebration and worship of Christ. Only in corporate worship do we grasp the excitement and the awe of that vision of heaven. We are surrounded by the love of our fellow Christians; we raise our voices in song and prayer together; we hear the Word of God through preaching. As we gather in Christ's name, the Holy Spirit moves among us—connecting, inspiring, and leading. It is unlikely that a Christian who regularly experiences such group worship will grow cold and defeated.

Elements of worship. Services vary from church to church. Most contain music, Scripture reading, preaching, offering, and prayer. Others might include announcements, business, sharing from the congregation of prayer concerns and praises, or such special features as communion or baptism. Your pastor and worship leaders put great effort into planning worship that will touch your life and direct your thoughts to God. The different parts of the service will gain more and more meaning as you continue to attend. Listen carefully and enter in wholeheartedly.

Worship Tips

1. Take your Bible to every service.

2. Sit near the front where distractions are minimized.

3. Center your thoughts on Jesus. Use the prelude time to pray and meditate.

4. If you are not familiar with the songs, turn to them in the hymn book anyway and try to learn them.

5. Go equipped to write down sermon notes, prayer requests, and instructions from the Holy Spirit.

6. Don't be afraid to share a praise or prayer request with the congregation if the service includes sharing time.

"*I rejoiced with those who said to me, 'Let us go to the house of the Lord.'* "

Psalm 122:1

Is worship taking or giving? As Christians, we value the benefits of worship services—good music and preaching, closeness with others, inner healing, the beauty of the sanctuary, and so on. But a worship service is not a performance for the persons in the pews. It is true that in worship we minister to each other as a loving family. In addition, in corporate worship God can minister directly to us in our personal relationship. In these ways, we are recipients during worship.

But our corporate worship should primarily honor Christ for who he is and what he has done. Our act of worship involves communicating to God our sense of awe and gratitude for Christ's sacrifice on the cross. While we realize in worship that God is our closest friend, we also bow down before him as the only majestic, all powerful Creator and Judge of the universe. Our worship must center on God and his Son, Jesus Christ.

Thus we come away from worship sensing that we have received of God's goodness. Chances are that worship will "do something for us." We will be fed and uplifted. But we should also come into a worship service already full from a week in close communication with God, and eager to give to him praise and thanks. Corporate worship is our chance to join with persons who have similarly experienced his miraculous love in their everyday lives. This combining of our joy in the Lord is an experience beyond description. You will want to enter into it with regularity.

☑ Check It Out

1. Being close to God is as essential to us as our most basic physical needs. The psalm writer expressed it this way: "As the deer pants for _____ _____." (Psalm 42:1-2 OT)

2. How or when do these Scripture passages say to spend time with God?

   Psalm 5:3 OT (a) _____

   Daniel 6:10 OT (b) _____

   Matthew 6:6 NT (c) _____

   Matthew 14:22-23 NT (d) _____

   Mark 1:35 NT (e) _____

3. God is eager to give us (a) _____ and (b) _____ when we approach him. (Hebrews 4:16 NT)

4. God (a) _____ us. We can call upon him as long as (b) _____ _____. (Psalm 116:1-2 OT)

5. David said that he _____ _____ at the thought of going to God's house. (Psalm 122:1 OT)

6. In the picture of heavenly worship, living beings praised God
day and night, giving him (a) ——————————————,
(b) ———————————, and (c) ——————————————.
(Revelation 4:9 NT. This is the last book in the Bible.)

7. List several things Christians are to do together.
(Ephesians 5:18-19 NT) (a) ——————————————

_____

_____

(Acts 2:42-47 NT) (b) ——————————————

_____

_____

_____

 Talk It Over

1. What are some differences between going to church and worshiping?
2. Do you think the setting or place of worship makes a difference? Why or why not?
3. If you have recently attended a worship service, what particularly spoke to you? Was there anything said or done that you did not understand? What?
4. Talk about some things you can think about or do before the next service that will make worship more meaningful for you.

6

Being an Overcomer

So far we have talked about many wonderful aspects of being a Christian. We have spoken of the Christian life as a daily walk with God with salvation as the starting point. We grow as Christians into the person God desires us to be by continuing to seek a closeness with God and his people.

Prayer, Bible study, fellowship, and worship are necessary ingredients of our new lives. But they are not guaranteed to prevent or cure every problem in life. Although God blesses us richly, we are not to expect perfect lives on this earth, free from troubles. We will still face doubt, temptation, and fear—problems that are common to everyone. But as Christians, we have adequate resources to deal with them.

Dealing with doubt

If you are feeling very good about becoming a Christian, enjoy every minute of it. You have made a life-changing commitment to God, and he is pleased and honors that decision. But don't be too surprised if, at some point, questions start to creep into your thinking.

Some questions might have to do with your salvation, such as "Was it real?" Others may be posed by friends or family members who try to convince you that your decision is meaningless. Other doubts may come in the form of questions that people all through the ages have struggled with, such as "Why does God allow suffering?"

God does not reject us when we have questions. Our searching lets God know that we care and want to come closer to him. The trick is to keep our questions from becoming destructive doubt, and from causing us to reject God or his people. In times when life seems at its worst, remember that saving faith was (and is) an act of your whole being. In your heart, you responded to the love of God, a love for you that will never change. In your mind, you accepted the suffering and death and resurrection of Christ. No amount of doubt will change the fact that Jesus is alive. Finally, in your will, you renounced sin and turned to God. Remember with patient thanksgiving what God has done for you and the inheritance he is preparing for you in heaven. Your doubts will fade.

If you recognize common doubts as not unique to yourself, that may help you have patience in dealing with them. Also remember that answers to some questions may remain obscured as long as you live. Consider the possibility that God wants us to continue to search. He wants us to be in a live relationship with other Christians, in which we discuss together and probe the Scriptures. On some questions we arrive together at conclusions on which we can act. On others, we ultimately admit that God's mind is far superior to our own. So we find it easier than non-Christians to leave some questions on "the back burner" and trust God to answer them in time or eternity. This is called faith.

Dealing with temptation

Sooner or later as a Christian, you will have thoughts which, if carried into practice, become sin. These initial stirrings are called temptations. As a Christian, you now have access to God's "armor" which protects you from succumbing to improper thoughts. Should we fail to equip ourselves against sin or to win the war against it, we have a provision for the restoration of our

*"The world and its desires
pass away, but the man
who does the will of God
lives forever."*

1 John 2:17

relationship with God (confession, forgiveness, cleansing). But we need to take very seriously three sources of evil and their possible effects on us.

The world. There eventually will be times at your job, or in the community, or even at home, when you feel out of place. This uncomfortable feeling is the result of the extreme difference between Christian attitudes and those of most other people. While most will search for security in possessions or accomplishments, you will have found yours in God. While others see no need for God, you will someday not be able to imagine life without him. While others use the name of your Savior as a mere exclamation in conversation, you will cringe at such a reference to the person whom you love so deeply. You will work for peace while others love war. You will want to obey God's laws, but others will blatantly break them. While others spend time and resources on extravagant entertainment, you will seek happiness in service.

As you remain close to God, you will feel a separateness from the ignorant and evil practices of the world because you now belong to the kingdom of Christ. At the same time, you will feel compassion for those who do not know Christ as you do. Christians are always caught in this tension of being "in" the world, but not "of" it. We need to be among people as a witness to Christ's power, but we must not yield to the temptation to be like the world in its practices and attitudes.

The flesh. When we become Christians, we change. Our spiritual life is awakened. We are born into eternal life. Our new nature, controlled by the Holy Spirit in us, opens the door to right living. It is the gift of God the Father, who created this new aspect of who we are when we confessed Jesus Christ as our Savior.

Yet the Bible clearly teaches that we have an enemy within. Many of the struggles we encounter are results of this old sinful part of us wanting to be in control again. Our old self, inherited from Adam and Eve, wants to rule and fights against obeying God. "The devil made me do it" is the easy excuse of those who do not recognize that they still have the inclination to sin. But the good news is that Christ makes available to us all the power we need to overrule our sinful tendencies.

The devil. Satan is a real being. He is devious and cruel, with the purpose of breaking our peaceful relationship with God and other human beings. Satan will try to drive wedges of hate and distrust between Christians. We need to view him as a real threat and remind ourselves in many situations that he is the real enemy, not our neighbor or God.

Satan was successful in leading the human race away from God in the first place. He eventually attacks every Christian. He wants you to doubt and forsake God. But because of Jesus' death and resurrection, Satan does not have the upper hand, and someday will be imprisoned forever. If we believe that Jesus conquered death—the ultimate weapon of Satan—then we can be victorious in daily situations over him and his many helpers through the power of Christ.

Dealing with fear

Fear is not sin, any more than temptation is. But fear can have a paralyzing effect on us if we do not confront it. Often fear is linked with the memory of suffering or trouble. We fear the effects of pain and adversity. We fear embarrassment, death, or the loss of security, loved ones, influence, or health. Christians often fear confrontation, telling others about our faith, or ridicule

> *"Peace I leave with you;*
> *my peace I give you.*
> *I do not give to you as the world gives.*
> *Do not let your hearts be troubled*
> *and do not be afraid."*
>
> John 14:27

and cruelty. We fear failure. Some Christians try overly hard to please God because they fear rejection by God himself.

Fear is normal and manageable. As you mature in your relationship with your heavenly Father, you will discover that the abundant life which God desires for you is one of peace and contentment despite what is going on around you. While certain fears are helpful, born into us and taught to us for our own protection, other damaging fears can be dissolved when we realize we are permanently in the arms of a loving, protecting God.

Release from fear is available. First, go directly to God. Pray. Tell God about your anxieties; tell him you trust him and thank him for everything; and ask him to relieve your fears. Go to the Bible and study the comforting words of promise there. Find specific ones which speak to your particular fears. Second, go to the church—the people of God. They can pray for you, love you, be an example of faith for you, and help you through your crises. Surround yourself with Christ's "love ambassadors." Their joy and hope will be contagious.

The privilege of victory

God desires that we be holy as he is holy. Yet while facing doubt, fear, and temptation, we will occasionally fail to be all that

God wants us to be. The wonderful and unique thing about being a Christian is that we do not need to remain defeated. Perhaps you will disappoint God and strain your relationship with him. But you still will have the privilege of being his child. He will listen as you approach him for forgiveness if you do not repeatedly and blatantly act irresponsibly and out of evil motives.

If we confess our shortcomings, God has promised not to hold them against us because Jesus has already paid the penalty for us. We may need to pay the earthly consequences for what we have done. That may include punishment and restoring what we have damaged. But our status with God is unchanged after we confess and turn from sin.

When you have doubts, temptations, or fears, the best thing you can do is deal with them immediately. Don't let them eat away at your joy. Identify them, pray about them, and confess them to a Christian friend if the situation calls for it. Then trust God to help you overcome them. Remember that Christ lived on earth as a human being and faced every possible trial that you face. You can rely on him to understand and help you.

Dealing with Temptation

1. Read the Bible and pray. Remember God's faithfulness to you and others in the past and believe God has the same power *now*.

2. Worship the God who can give you power to reject the temptation. Cleanse your mind with the healing effects of Christian music.

3. Avoid tempting situations.

4. Be accountable to another Christian in dealing with recurring temptations.

Check It Out

If you are thinking that the questions are getting tougher, you're right! Keep digging and praying that the Holy Spirit will help you understand. You'll be amazed how good you'll be at this in just a short while. If you do get "stuck," don't be discouraged. God will reveal to you in time all you need to know.

1. Our confidence in God increases as we learn more about who God is. List some of God's characteristics:

   (Genesis 1:1 OT and John 1:1-3 NT)

   (a) _____

   (Psalm 103:8 OT) (b) _____

   (c) _____

   (d) _____

   (e) _____

   (Jeremiah 23:24 OT) (f) _____

   (Revelation 1:8 NT) (g) _____

2. Who is our High Priest, was tempted just as we are, and is able to help us? (Hebrews 4:14-15 NT) _____

3. What three-fold comfort does 1 Corinthians 10:13 (NT) give us about temptation?

   (a) _____

   (b) _____

   (c) _____

continued on next page

4. In John 17:15 (NT), Jesus prays that God will set us apart and protect us, but not take us out of the _____.

5. God is the father of Christians. The father of non-Christians is the devil. List some of his characteristics or actions.

(John 8:44 NT) (a) _____

(b) _____

(Ephesians 2:2 NT) (c) _____

(d) _____

(1 John 3:8 NT) (e) _____

6. Who has greater power—God or Satan? (1 John 4:4 NT)

_____

7. We should resist the devil's schemes and he will _____ _____. (James 4:7 NT)

8. The Apostle Paul claimed to have learned the secret of (a) _____. (Philippians 4:11-13 NT) Write out his secret from verse 13.

(b) _____

_____

9. What did Jesus say to do about our fear of lacking material possessions? (Matthew 6:33 NT) _____

_____

10. Trials and testing come so that our faith can be purified and proven precious, strong, and genuine. Our victory over troubles results in (a) ——————, (b) ——————, and (c) —————————————— to Christ. (1 Peter 1:7 NT)

11. We can be (a) —————————— when we face trials because trials help us develop (b) ——————————————————. (James 1:2-3 NT)

12. Read Romans 8:35-39 (NT). When we come to Christ, can anything separate us from God's love? ——————————————

 Talk It Over

1. Try reading and putting into your own words Hebrews 10:35-39, Hebrews 13:5-6, and James 1:2-6.

2. If temptations have cropped up in your life, try to figure out the source (world, your own self, Satan). How will you deal with these temptations? Who will win if you rely on Christ?

3. Are you experiencing any fears? What are they? What help and advice are found in Philippians 4:4-8?

7

Telling Others

As you progress on your Christian journey, you soon will want to tell other people what has happened to you. This is called *witnessing*. Just as witnesses in a courtroom tell truthfully what they have seen or heard, you will want to pass on to others the changes you are experiencing and what you now know about Jesus Christ. You are a Christian today because someone, somehow told you. Believe it or not, as you are faithful, God can bring someone else to Christ through your witness.

Why tell others?

Imagine that you have a million dollar debt that is making life very difficult. Then one day someone walks into the bank and pays off your loan in its entirety. The weight of worry is now lifted. Wouldn't you want to run to friends, family, and even strangers to tell them about the loving and kind deed this person has done? Our situation as Christians is much the same. When Jesus Christ died on the cross, our sin debt was stamped "paid in full." What's more, his resurrection has given us eternal life. You and I now know by experience this story of redemption. It is a precious treasure which cannot be hidden.

The Bible says that when our hearts are full, our mouths speak. When the Holy Spirit enters our lives, joy wells up within us. We become fuller and fuller until the good news spills out to all around. The Apostle Paul uses another image. He says that the gospel is like a sweet perfume. Think what the world could be like if each Christian put forth the fragrance of the gospel in word and deed!

Christ told his followers to go out and proclaim the good news to all people, teaching and baptizing them. In fact, this "telling" is commanded all through Scripture. God certainly could have used any means he wanted to let people know about his power and love. But he chose to have us tell each other. The Holy Spirit is busy preparing people's hearts to receive the Truth. But we are to be the way the message is made known.

How do I tell?

Remember what life was like before you met Christ? Don't ever forget that. In fact, as soon as you can, write down what happened, or put it on tape. You will want to recall every detail, so make it as long as you wish. Perhaps someone could help you. Or, if you are not comfortable with writing or speaking, simply compile three short paragraphs on these topics: (1) what my life was like before I believed in Jesus, (2) what the circumstances were surrounding my confession of faith, and (3) what changes I have already noticed in my life. This account, preserved for you, will help as you tell your story to others, and be a reminder in years to come of those first wonderful moments of salvation.

Somewhere along the way, training in evangelism will be helpful. But for now, you don't need a course in witnessing before you can tell someone about Christ. The Bible says that talking about God is a daily event—starting today. Christians do not confine their religion to inside the church walls on Sunday. We see God's hand in everyday situations. Because we meet him in many places and many ways, our daily experiences together with God's Word confirm his goodness and presence. As you find this

"But in your hearts set apart Christ as Lord. Always be prepared to give an answer to everyone who asks you to give reason for the hope you have. But do this with gentleness and respect. . . ."

1 Peter 3:15-16

to be true, talk about it. Tell it to your family, friends, other Christians, or anyone who seems to have an ear to listen.

Christian witness involves both conduct and words. Your changed behavior will confirm your words when you speak. But you must not wait until you are perfect to verbally witness. You'll wait forever. By conscientious living, prayer, time studying the Bible, and a close walk with God, you prepare to sow the seed of faith in someone else when opportunities arise.

Speak gently, respectfully, and humbly. You may talk to someone unashamedly because your message is true. Always be boldly alert for chances to share. But don't be rude or too forceful. Keep Christ the central person in your message, not yourself. Remember that your circumstances were unique, and so will be those of the other person. Be adaptable. Most importantly, love, love, love. Tell people what God is doing in your life, then leave the matter in God's hands.

Should I expect results?

If you obediently witness, allowing the Holy Spirit to give you the words to say, you will undoubtedly feel good afterwards. God created us to honor him. When we verbally attest to his greatness, we not only please God, but we confirm our own salvation. There is an assurance which follows witnessing that is distinctively full of pleasure. The joy comes from merely speaking the gospel, not necessarily from immediate results or a warm reception. Not everyone who hears you will come to the Lord. Some may even cruelly make fun of you. You are not responsible for the free choice of others. Don't be discouraged.

But when your testimony does lead a person to Christ through confession of faith, be assured that the angels in heaven rejoice with you at this wonderful event. You are blessed because you have been obedient. And the newly saved person now has eternal life. What a privilege it is to be the vehicle for God's grace as well as the recipient. Those who keep silent will never know this kind of joy.

Another result of your public testimony will be your confirmation as a member of the body of Christ. When you openly confess your belief in Christ as your Savior and Lord before the church, you take on the privileges of full membership in a local congregation. Baptism, which often accompanies public confession of faith, is a great moment in the life of the believer and the church. These acts of testimony, love, and commitment verify what has happened in your life.

So, Christian, be encouraged. You can be sure your salvation is real. You now know how to begin your daily walk with God. You realize that doubts, fears, and temptations are normal and need not overcome you. And you can step out in faith to tell others about Jesus Christ. Your new life has begun!

☑ Check It Out

1. As Christians, we are Christ's _____.
   (2 Corinthians 5:20 NT)

2. Write down Jesus' first and last commands to the disciples:
   (Mark 1:17 NT) (a) _____

   _____

   (Mark 16:15) (b) _____

   _____

3. How can people be saved if they have never _____
   of Jesus? (Romans 10:14 NT)

4. Where is there rejoicing when one person comes to believe in
   Jesus? _____ (Luke 15:10 NT)

5. If our hearts are full of the good news of God, it will overflow
   into what we _____ . (Luke 6:45 NT)

6. When Moses tried to make excuses so he would not have to
   speak to Pharaoh, God replied, "Now go, I will _____

   _____

   _____."

   (Exodus 4:10-12 OT. This is the second book of the Bible.)

7. We should always be _____ with an answer if
   asked about our faith. (1 Peter 3:15-16 NT)

continued on next page

8. We need to _____ for those who are witnessing. (Colossians 4:3-4 NT)

9. The light of Christ which shines in the lives of Christians is a valuable _____ which we should share. (2 Corinthians 4:6-7 NT)

10. Our good _____ are (is) also part of our witness. (1 Peter 2:12 NT)

11. Presenting the gospel to people is compared to scattering _____. (Luke 8:4-15 NT; Psalm 126:6 OT)

12. Not all the seeds will grow into believers, but Jesus said, " _____

_____." (Matthew 9:37 NT)

13. What can you say to a non-believer who:
    (a) believes his good works can save him? (Ephesians 2:8-9 NT)

    _____

    _____

    (b) thinks people from any belief or religion are going to heaven? (John 14:6 and Acts 4:12 NT)

    _____

    (c) believes Christians are hypocrites? (Romans 14:12 NT)

    _____

(d) says, "I'll commit myself someday, but not yet." (2 Corinthians 6:2; James 4:13-14 NT)

 # Talk It Over

1. Who are some of the people you can tell what has happened to you?
2. Read 1 Corinthians 15:1-4 and Mark 5:19. Then try to say or write a brief testimony including the basic Christian good news and your own story.
3. What warnings are found for us in 1 Corinthians 4:1-6?
4. Discuss how you might feel and what you might do if someone makes fun of you when you tell him or her about Christ.
5. Talk about the step of baptism and what it will mean to you in your Christian walk.

"Now to him who is able to do immeasurably more than all we ask or imagine, according to his power that is at work within us, to him be glory in the church and in Christ Jesus throughout all generations, for ever and ever! Amen."

Ephesians 3:20-21

Six-Week Bible Reading Plan

If you need a way to start reading the Bible, try these three two-week plans.

Two weeks on the life and teachings of Jesus
- [ ] Day 1. Luke 1: Preparing for Jesus' arrival
- [ ] Day 2. Luke 2: The story of Jesus' birth
- [ ] Day 3. Mark 1: The beginning of Jesus' ministry
- [ ] Day 4. Mark 9: A day in the life of Jesus
- [ ] Day 5. Matthew 5: The Sermon on the Mount
- [ ] Day 6. Matthew 6: The Sermon on the Mount
- [ ] Day 7. Luke 15: Parables of Jesus
- [ ] Day 8. John 3: A conversation with Jesus
- [ ] Day 9. John 14: Jesus' final instructions
- [ ] Day 10. John 17: Jesus' prayer for his disciples
- [ ] Day 11. Matthew 26: Betrayal and arrest
- [ ] Day 12. Matthew 27: Jesus' execution on a cross
- [ ] Day 13. John 20: Resurrection
- [ ] Day 14. Luke 24: Jesus' appearance after resurrection

Two weeks on salvation
- [ ] Day 1. Genesis 3: The first sin creates a need
- [ ] Day 2. Isaiah 52: Salvation prophesied
- [ ] Day 3. Isaiah 53: The role of the suffering servant
- [ ] Day 4. Luke 15: Three stories about God's love
- [ ] Day 5. John 3: Jesus explains "born again"
- [ ] Day 6. John 10: The good shepherd
- [ ] Day 7. Acts 8: Conversions spread outside the Jews
- [ ] Day 8. Acts 26: Paul testifies of his conversion before a king
- [ ] Day 9. Romans 3: God's provision for sin
- [ ] Day 10. Romans 5: Peace with God
- [ ] Day 11. Galatians 3: Unavailable through obeying the law
- [ ] Day 12. Ephesians 2: New life in Christ
- [ ] Day 13. 1 Peter 1: Future rewards of salvation
- [ ] Day 14. 2 Peter 1: Making sure of salvation

Two weeks on prayers of the Bible

☐ Day 1. Genesis 18: Abraham's plea for Sodom
☐ Day 2. Exodus 15: Moses' song to the Lord
☐ Day 3. Exodus 33: Moses meets with God
☐ Day 4. 2 Samuel 7: David's response to God's promises
☐ Day 5. 1 Kings 8: Solomon's dedication of the temple
☐ Day 6. 2 Chronicles 20: Jehoshaphat prays for victory
☐ Day 7. Ezra 9: Ezra's prayer for the people's sins
☐ Day 8. Psalm 22: A cry to God for help
☐ Day 9. Psalm 104: A prayer of praise
☐ Day 10. Daniel 9: Daniel's prayer for the salvation of Jerusalem
☐ Day 11. Habbakkuk 3: A prophet's prayer of acceptance
☐ Day 12. Matthew 6: The Lord's prayer
☐ Day 13. John 17: Jesus' prayer for his disciples
☐ Day 14. Colossians 1: Paul's prayer of thanksgiving

Reprinted by permission from *The Student Bible: New International Version,* published by Zondervan Bible Publishers, Grand Rapids, Michigan.

Other two-week tracks are available in *The Student Bible.* This Bible also lists a six-month track; an overview of the entire Bible; and a three-year track, to read all the way through the Bible.

Prayer Journal

These pages are provided for you to list your prayer requests and the answers. Also list praises.

Date   *Prayers and praises*   *Date and Answer*

_____

_____

_____

_____

_____

_____

_____

_____

_____

_____

_____

_____

_____

_____

_____

_____

_____

Date   *Prayers and praises*   *Date and Answer*

Answers

Chapter 1

1. new person or creature or creation
2. (a) strengthen
   (b) loves
3. peace
4. eternal or everlasting life
5. rest
6. fears
7. forgive us
8. (a) love
   (b) children or sons
   (c) God
9. (a) obey or keep his commandments; or try to do what God wants
   (b) love one another
   (c) have God's Holy Spirit

   (b) doctrine or teaching (the truth)
   (c) reproof; or to make us realize what is wrong in our lives; or refuting, or correcting error
   (d) correction; or straightening us out; or resetting direction
   (e) instruction or training in righteousness or right, good, or holy living; helping us do what is right
4. disciples
5. opens
6. the Holy Spirit or Spirit of truth
7. "Open my eyes that I may see the wonderful things in your law."
8. so we won't sin
9. do or obey

Chapter 2

1. confidence or boldness
2. (a) anxious or worried or careful (full of cares)
   (b) peace
3. good gifts or good things
4. (a) obey him or keep his commandments
   (b) please
5. (a) alone or in secret
   (b) small
   (c) large
6. temptation
7. (a) early in the morning
   (b) night or evening
   (c) all night

Chapter 3

1. foolishness
2. higher
3. (a) given by inspiration from God, or God-breathed, or inspired by God

Chapter 4

1. praise, or glorify, or give glory to
2. encourage
3. gathering together (If you gave more information, that's fine.)
4. body
5. (Don't worry on this one if your answers are slightly different. Just remember that there are many.)
   contributing to others; faith; healing; serving; leading; pastoring; doing miraculous things; teaching; showing mercy; wisdom; ability to speak in and interpret tongues; encouraging; being an evangelist; knowledge; ability to distinguish between spirits
6. mature or perfect
7. (a) love one another
   (b) live in harmony, are sympathetic, and love as brothers
   (c) bear (share) one another's burdens or troubles

Chapter 5

1. (This answer is from the NIV.
   Yours may be a bit different.)
   streams of water, so my soul pants
   for you, O God
2. (a) every morning
   (b) kneeling, three times a day
   (c) in private or secret
   (d) alone (in the hills)
   (e) alone, before daybreak
3. (a) mercy
   (b) grace
4. (a) hears or listens to
   (b) we live or we breathe
5. rejoiced or was glad
6. (a) glory
   (b) honor
   (c) thanks
7. (a) be filled with the Holy Spirit,
   and speak to each other with
   psalms, hymns, and spiritual
   songs
   (b) teaching and fellowship; breaking of bread; prayer; wonders
   and miracles; shared everything; sold possessions and
   gave to the needy; met at the
   temple; ate; praised God.

Chapter 6

1. (a) Creator of everything
   (b) merciful or compassionate
   (c) gracious, or tender toward
   those who are undeserving
   (d) slow to anger
   (e) plenteous in mercy, abounding
   in or full of lovingkindness
   (f) no one can hide from God;
   God is everywhere at all times,
   or he fills heaven and earth

(g) God is Alpha and Omega
   (beginning and end), the all-
   powerful, almighty one who is
   coming again
2. Jesus the Son of God
3. (a) no temptation is unique to us
   (b) God will not let us be tempted
   beyond what we can bear
   (c) God has promised to provide a
   way to escape temptation's
   power
4. world
5. (a) murderer
   (b) liar
   (c) mighty and evil prince or ruler
   of the kingdom of the air (spiritual powers in space or the
   spiritual realm)
   (d) works in the hearts of (or con-
   trols) those who disobey God
   (e) has kept on sinning since the
   beginning
6. God
7. flee or run away
8. (a) contentment
   (b) I can do everything God asks
   me to with the help of Christ
   who gives me strength and
   power
9. Seek God's kingdom and righteousness first; or give God first
   place in your heart and life
10. (a) praise
   (b) glory
   (c) honor
11. (a) happy or joyful
   (b) patience, perseverance, endur-
   ance, fortitude, or steadfastness
12. No.

Chapter 7

1. ambassadors
2. (a) Come follow me and I will make you fishers of men.
   (b) Go into all the world and preach the good news (gospel) to all creation (everyone everywhere)
3. heard
4. in the presence of angels
5. say or speak
6. help you speak and teach you what to say
7. ready or prepared
8. pray
9. treasure
10. lives, works, deeds, or conduct
11. seed
12. The harvest is plentiful, but the workers are few.
13. (a) It is by grace (God's gift and kindness) that people are saved through faith . . . not by works, so that no one can boast. (In simpler words, salvation is not a reward for good things we have done. We are saved through trusting Christ.)
    (b) Jesus said, "No one comes to the Father except through me."
    (c) Each of us will give an account of himself to God.
    (d) Now is the day of salvation, for we don't know what tomorrow will bring or if tomorrow will come at all.

I, (name) _____ , completed this book on (date) _____ .

My friend, (name) _____ , helped me to begin my Christian life by working through my questions with me, and supporting me with kindness and prayer.